Blue Jesus

OTHER BOOKS BY JIM DANIELS
   Factory Poems
   On the Line
   Places/Everyone
   The Long Ball
   Digger's Territory
   Punching Out
   Hacking It
   M-80
   Niagara Falls
   Blessing the House
   No Pets

BOOKS EDITED BY JIM DANIELS
   Carnegie Mellon Anthology of Poetry
      (CO-EDITED WITH GERALD COSTANZO)
   Letters to America: Contemporary American Poetry
      on Race

Blue Jesus

Jim Daniels

CARNEGIE MELLON UNIVERSITY PRESS
PITTSBURGH 2000

ACKNOWLEDGMENTS

AMERICAN LITERARY REVIEW: "Hymns"
BIRMINGHAM POETRY REVIEW: "Self-Portrait with Watch"
BLOOMSBURY REVIEW: "Evolution: Two Figures with Monkey"
CAROLINA QUARTERLY: "Night Janitor, McMahon Oil"
CHICAGO REVIEW: "Spider Boy Killed in Massive Manhunt"
GLOBAL CITY REVIEW: "Snaked Man," "Haircut on the 21st
    Floor," "Water from a Tap"
KENYON REVIEW: "Shedding the Vestments"
KESTREL: "Angels Bowling on All Saints Day," "Crafts,"
    "Children of the Damned"
THE OHIO REVIEW: "Red Jesus," "White Jesus," "Blue Jesus"
PASSAGES NORTH: "Angels, Shmangels"
PERMAFROST: "The Fall"
WITNESS: "Yellow Jesus," "Silver Jesus"

"Hymns" also appeared in BROODING THE HEARTLANDS:
    POETS OF THE MIDWEST, M. L. Liebler, Editor, Bottom
    Dog Press, 1998.

"Night Janitor, McMahon Oil," also appeared in HACKING IT,
    a chapbook from Ridgeway Press, 1992.

Many of the poems in this book—and all of those in section
three—were written in response to the paintings of Francis
Bacon. In section three, the title of the painting appears in
italics beneath the poem's title.

The publication of this book is supported by a grant from the
Pennsylvania Council on the Arts.

Library of Congress Catalog Card Number 99-74768
ISBN 0-88748-332-1
Copyright © 2000 by Jim Daniels
All rights reserved
Printed and bound in the United States of America

10 9 8 7 6 5 4 3 2 1

CONTENTS

3. *(con't)*

1.

YELLOW JESUS

Can you keep a secret?
I have seen haloes around the heads
of beautiful women. Okay, shoot me
with a well-intentioned folk song—
I'm telling the truth
till it hurts: I love the body.
I love the sonic boom boom
of the heart after skin touches skin.

•

When I was young and my pores
clogged with pure impurity,
I took pleasure in squeezing out
the pus, though you're not supposed
to squeeze. We all know
the poison's in there. It was nice
to see some of it come out
now and then, and wipe it away,
and imagine I might live
thirty more good seconds.

•

We have stained the walls of churches
with candle smoke for a long time
and counting. A little bit of hell
to heat up the holy water. I try to keep
the faith *and* keep the fires burning.

•

Yellow Jesus,
is the sun Your good eye,
and the moon Your evil eye?
Some mornings I stand naked at the window
while my favorite saint sleeps on,
and I see them both in the clear blue,
my two yellow friends,
and I could believe in anything.

Blue Jesus

RED JESUS

I see Him in the struck match
and in the dead leaf wandering, stepped on.
He burns my ears with the angry pulse
of what I don't understand. He lives
in the clenched. He is the knock at the door
when I do not wish. He is the red fingers.
He is not blood but what causes blood
to appear. I miss Him even when
I am gently brushing a stranger's hair.
He can hold his breath longer than anyone.
His throne is the electric chair. His every vowel
is a contest, and we're stepping on
each other's throats to get the medals.
Even as I sleep, my fingers curl inward
on His smile.

GREEN JESUS

has been erased from the hymnals
and turned into a three-prong outlet.
The lustful priest hid Him in his guitar
at the folk mass, but no one was fooled.
His sweat nourished the rectory's house plant
while they broke him down and he confessed.
Back to the organ's stomp and shriek.
Green Jesus guzzles poison, then reappears
between sidewalk cracks. Green Jesus
of the hillside and meadow, the smooth curve,
the beautiful chaos. He accepts no folded letters.
He says *why not admit your ignorance?*
He whispers *this is as loud as it gets*. The lustful
priest happily goes deaf. Green Jesus stains the knees
of the blessed children. When you call Him,
He does not answer. He is sarcasm's greatest enemy.
He is the circular prayer, the spinning wheel.
We make our money green. We call green lucky.
We call it inexperienced. We scrub it out.

BLUE JESUS

Sleepless, and the clock hands
throbbing. I have to get on the red phone
to the Blue Jesus of my dreams
and say *help* or *squeak* or *who was*
that monster at my office door,
Satan or the ghost of J. Edgar Hoover?

Blue Jesus smears the ink of my dreams,
wandering like the ridiculous cape
of the artist-wannabe at a dull party—
beautiful, no matter who wears it.

I'm knocking at His door.
It's pretty dark in there. Maybe it comes down
to trusting the mirages, the shadows,
the unfinished

PURPLE JESUS

Jesus, I'm not done with You.
Are You done with me?
Last week I stopped in a church
to look at a box they say
holds some holy bones
just to say I was there.

You have to take it on faith
that I was there, that I saw the box,
that the bones were in the box,
that the bones were St. Valentine's,
that St. Valentine was a holy man,
holy enough to join the frat,
that the people who let him in
weren't fools to begin with,
filling each other's underwear
with shaving cream.
You see what I'm saying?
I haven't even got anywhere near
what it takes to believe in You.

•

I walked in to the smell
of Purple Jesus
rising in sweet incense
like one beautiful letter
repeating itself above our heads.
Purple Jesus makes me shut up
and admire the dust I'm headed for.

My mother can't kneel anymore.
She sits during the kneeling parts—
on the edge of the pew so she's not quite
comfortable, so her knees almost
touch the kneeler. She believes

the somber Purple Jesus knows
she'd be kneeling
if it didn't hurt
quite so much.

•

Purple Jesus, my favorite crayon.
You don't make me a soldier
in Your army. You don't ask for
the numb repeated prayer.
You simply want my sadness.

I go in churches as a tourist
to look at art made in Your name.
One Good Friday I stood in back
with my arms crossed, and an angry
man made me unfold them.
If that's all it takes
to dis You,
I'm in trouble.

•

We don't get to see the Purple Jesus
very often, though when I smoked
a lot of pot, I imagined I saw Him often.

I meant no disrespect.
I mean no disrespect.
Lord have Mercy.
Christ have Mercy.

If I was going to rise from the dead,
spring would be the time.
I am writing a name in the layered sunset.
Mine, not His.

SILVER JESUS

The sun turns olive leaves
into reflecting silver medals
like the ones I wore around
my neck. They bounced
against my young thump
as I ran the bases.
I stayed on the worn paths,
I rested on the dirty sacks.
Safe, I was safe.

Olive leaves don't turn.
They don't fall off. And You, Silver
Jesus, dead at 33. Old, I used to think.
My hair is nearly all gray, but silver
sounds better, as if it had value.
How can you feel old if you're going
to live forever?

That's the sort of thing that stops me,
even now. How much gray hair did
You have? The medals tarnished
over time. One day they slid
into a bottomless drawer.

Wherever we stand, we're never safe.
Okay, okay, I am not wise, and my knees hurt.
I don't know which way to bend,
or whether to kneel at all. Olive leaves
shimmer around me in the bright sun.
I take my gray head and my creaking limbs
out among the gnarled trunks. I twirl.

ORANGE JESUS

We all see the skin.
The question is
whether the juice exists.
If I grind at the rind long enough,
maybe I'll scrape my way through.
I hope it's okay to go this route
instead of folding my hands
bowing my head
and telling my favorite lies.

•

A young man bounces a ball
down my concrete street.
The echo equals half a gunshot.
Excuse me for being so precise—
it's what the city demands.

When he stares at me
I stare back until my eyes
lose focus. Between us
the angry sound waves
of that orange ball waver in heat.

•

Smile for the camera,
smile for the camera,
Orange Jesus snapping the picture
for His scrapbook of lost causes,
the flash erupting—one blinding moment.
It's a relief to stop smiling
and ease back into hell.

•

I believe that orange ball is filled
with air. It's got a slow leak.
I keep pumping, pumping.
Orange Jesus, do You really love me
like everybody says?

•

I am an orange dog yipping against
the random length of chain.
Orange Jesus, don't lose patience
with my wandering. One day I hope
to get lost enough
to find You.

•

I swallow the bitter rind.
I am learning the meaning of thirst.

•

Half a gunshot, half a dropped hymnal
in an empty church. The orange edges
of the pages, flapping, settling.

•

I slice open an old basketball
and slip it over my head
to feel the awkward darkness
of a halo.

BROWN JESUS

Brown Jesus, dust of the earth,
how do we keep from choking?

dry throat coated
dark moon under the nails
wet mud of the liquid heart
the sun's idea of faith
pure smudge on a child's face
cut hair falling to earth

Brown Jesus
smudge my face
with the sound of grit

Brown Jesus
keep me here
pinched between Your fingers

tobacco before burning
sin before ignition

Brown Jesus, will You burn
into my favorite ash? Or will I?

I have faith in the dark sound
of a hollow-bodied guitar
but what if it moves me
to dance?

Brown Jesus, I'm rounding
third, headed for home

I'm going to slide
I'm going to at least
kick up a cloud

Blue Jesus

WHITE JESUS

is only visible to the naked eye.
Smells like bleach and soap
and sperm, the clean ironed cloth
of ceremony.

White Jesus is a theory. The fifth base.
The finger pointing into space.
The wall of unspoken apology.
The shirt worn to funerals.

My young children wrapped in towels
after a bath, waiting to be lifted up.
A white sheet blown horizontal,
clothespins holding tight

against the myth of rising up
if only they'd let go.

2.

PRAYING MAN TURNS HIMSELF IN FOR CRIMES UNCOMMITTED

My batteries are charged with belief,
positive on positive. The church will not
return my phone calls. They suspect
I will fry their fuses. The priest's
yellow hum sticks like bad gum
so what am I supposed to do, listen?
After you praise all the animals and plants,
you still have to eat a hamburger. I kneel
on the sidewalk in front of the old Italian's shrine
to St. Anthony with Car Reflectors. Even he
does not see the genius of his auto shrine
for the plaster saint. He chases me with a broken
broomstick and stutters curses. The police laugh
when they are called. I will laugh when I am called,
telling Jesus how I saw his face in oil stains
and soiled rags, how I fashioned communion wafers
from Wonder Bread and made a neon crucifix.
It is true, I am the smoking gun.
Here is my tattooed confession.

ANGELS, SHMANGELS

Last night the baby wouldn't sleep,
tears flying. This morning
the dog clatters against the wood floor
next to the bed, rancid panting
in my face. He wants out,
or he'll piss on the floor.

When he dreams, it's a comfort to know
the limited possibilities inside
his clunky brain. But what's he chasing?
High-pitched yips he never makes awake
trill beneath the loose flap of his jowl.

The baby sleeps now. He'll need a new diaper
when he wakes. It was nice to believe
in angels, to imagine their soft wings.
I taste the bitter dreams
of the money I'm going to need.

My wife sleeps off the night's
tension, another child alive
inside her. She needs the extra
rest. We will need the dream
money. Our window fan blows
over us, the breath of a minor god.

Phone's ringing. Who calls
so early? The dog dances over
to my wife's side, then back.
I rise slowly onto the heavy feet
of this life. Wings,
they'd just be a nuisance.

ANGELS BOWLING ON ALL SAINTS DAY

The rain is falling
and the leaves are falling
like used calendar pages,
and my son who's one—he's
got a digit now, he's in
the record book—is coughing
like he's official. I'm trying
to teach him the word *phlegm*
but he keeps saying *Jim*.
I'm holding his hand and talking
about electricity and dreams.

Walking to school, my brother and I
discussed the bowling scores of angels,
the names of their alleys—
Strikes in Paradise, Heavenly Lanes,
Spares a Plenty.
                    It's All Saints Day
and I'm putting my sweater on inside out
and reciting a litany of my dead.
Everybody who dies is a saint—
that's part of my religion.
Otherwise, I get confused
about who decides and how.

I've got the sniffles,
a gift from the kid with the digit.
Yesterday we crunched leaves, threw
them in the air. We sat in cold dirt
and smiled for no reason.
                    The older
you get, the more you need
a reason. Today we're just looking
out the window at the rain, the gray

skies of the first cold month. Some-
body told me angels are making a come-
back. Come back? Where'd they go?

Do they have computerized scoring
in heaven now? That's a point
I'd bring up with my brother
if he were still around.
They all sound like strikes today—
lightning splits a tree in the woods
out back. Maybe it's heaven I smell,
electricity and smoke. The kid
coughs, angels bowling in his chest.

Most people put an x in the box
to mark a strike. I color in
the whole square. I love being filled,
like I am today, with love for my sick child.

So, if the angels are bowling, then
who's crying? Who's losing? The rain falls
steady and objective.

Phlegm, I say, *Cough it up.*

CRAFTS

In Mrs. Baloff's class
we had to make something
useless. I glued paper
over a bent hanger, blended
paint till it was mud.
It was very useless.
It was a 'D'.
               Just like the 'D'
I got in handwriting from Sister
Lucy Anne—why was she so angry?
Because she couldn't read
my handwriting? Stanley
Bullock, who resembled a buffalo
in size and demeanor,
sat behind me and poked me
with his compass—I mean,
who could concentrate? We shared
the same kind of doubts. Bloody
pin points dotted the back of my shirt.

            •

I was proud that I had been
to both Paradise, and Hell,
Michigan, when my friends
had never even been to Canada.
They were both dumps
but I bought the postcards:
"I Been to Hell"
"I Been to Paradise."
I kept them in my desk
and fingered them during Religion.

            •

I shaped pieces of tinfoil
into coins and sealed them
in my church envelope, dropped them
in the collection basket.

Blue Jesus

Those ushers ripping open envelopes
in the rectory, watching football
with fat Father Frank, I bet
they got a kick out of that,
I bet they got an extra point
out of that.
                    Why was I so bitter
about God then, what had He done to me?
I got a 'D' in Conduct,
a 'D' in Effort and Study Habits.
D was my middle name,
D as in Dog, the one who died—
totally useless and I loved him.

"CHILDREN OF THE DAMNED"

with glowing zombie eyes—
kids from England in sissy suits—
zapping everyone who pissed them off
while we sat tight in our seats, in love
with screaming in the dark.

The Ryan Theater, forty cents
for kids under twelve. We stooped,
mussed our hair, smudged
our faces to look younger
than that kind of caring.

●

Randy Leemer sat down
next to me and my brother
at BEN-HUR. We cringed. Randy
smiled his giant simian grin,
a Jethro Bodine gone bad,
Jethro after losing his millions,
Jethro after his first dose of the clap.

The ushers threw us out
just for sitting next to him.
The ushers, the only ones tough enough
to get Randy out of a place he didn't want to leave,
angry high school dropouts making minimum wage,
hair greased back, waving their big flashlights
like they knew it'd be a long time
before those batteries wore down.

●

When I stopped going to church
I went to more movies, hanging out
in the shade under the marquee
waiting for the matinee. Damned,

I was damned and I knew it—
pale-skin summers in the cool darkness
where I was never blessed
but I was soothed
where I never took the sacraments
but I was filled.

•

The line for FLIPPER
curled past the doctor's office,
the barber shop, and around the theater,
everyone baking in that long line
for some stupid movie about a fish that was LASSIE.
I walked past, shook my head. In the alley behind A&P
we spit on the rubble and smoked cigarettes.
We were the chosen few
smashing bottles against the theater wall.

•

No one went to a movie alone with another guy
and we were afraid to ask girls
so we sat in groups of three or four,
punching each other to make sure we were okay.
And it had to be the right kind of movie
not some sissy thing like GIDGET GOES HAWAIIAN
or TO SIR WITH LOVE.

SOME OF US hadn't thrown out our plastic models
of GODZILLA and KING KONG and THE MUMMY
and DRACULA and CREATURE FROM THE BLACK LAGOON
and FRANKENSTEIN and MOTHRA and RODAN
and GIDRA THE THREE-HEADED MONSTER.

So, maybe we spent just a little too much time
with the glue and the little jars of paint.
So, maybe we were a little retarded
in our ability to converse with the opposite sex,

Blue Jesus

with girls, with them of the pretty hair
and sweet smells that turned our eyes to oats
and our hearts to little pads of butter,
real butter.

Yeah, well.

•

The owner pushed BUN BARS in the lobby
for double price. My pockets bulged
with candy heisted from the dime store
down the street. BUN BARS, magic brown squares
forty cents—the price of admission,
eight boxes of MILK DUDS. What was so good
about them? We never had enough money
to find out. We crammed our mouths
with GOOD 'N PLENTY, GOOBERS, RAISINETTES,
and MILK DUDS which tasted awful
and stuck to your teeth but lasted
a long time, unlike WHOPPERS
which disappeared in seconds,
though still better than JUICY FRUITS
which stuck to your teeth even longer
but tasted like hard jello.

We sat through those double features—
our teeth falling out into the aisles,
our pimples, when we got them,
popping. We were rotting in the dark,
loving the dark—rotting and loving.
Our shoes stuck to the cement floor,
the sticky affection we longed for—
it wanted us to stay.

•

Blue Jesus

GODZILLA was my champion—I liked his wit,
his air, debonair. Whatever happened
to those two tiny girls in the box
who called MOTHRA to the rescue?
My first sexual yearnings
were for those girls:
Let me be your MOTHRA baby.

Though MOTHRA was an ugly caterpillar
who spit some kind of goo. Looking back,
it seems kind of phallic
but maybe my memory is wrong
maybe I'm not so reliable
maybe I'm a CHILD OF THE DAMNED.

•

I was never scared
so why did I love them?
I wanted to eat skyscrapers,
stomp on cars, I wanted to make
a sandwich with my worst teachers inside
like Mr. Dabby, who was enormous
and liked to bounce me off the lockers
out in the hallway, who I called
the FLABBY DABBY MONSTER
and drew a picture of in class
that STEVE KURMAS (real name)
who is still somehow my friend
grabbed out of my hand as the bell rang
and said *Jim drew a picture of you,
MR. DABBY* and I had to have a meeting—
one of those meetings—with THE PRINCIPAL, MR. DABBY
and MY MOTHER, a meeting where my drawing
was not appreciated, though I incorporated
elements of KING KONG and GIDRA. Why did I do it,
they wanted to know, why? I had no excuse
and I was damned.

Blue Jesus

And like SISTER LUCY ANNE,
with her evil black RODAN-like wings,
her beakish nose and squawky voice.
She gave me D's in handwriting,
told me to practice crawling at home
to improve my writing. In front of the class.
In sixth grade. Practice crawling.
It was almost as bad as in eleventh grade
when I got sold at the Slave Auction Fundraiser
for only 90 cents and my friends started calling me
THE NINETY-CENT ASSHOLE. Remember, STEVE?

•

My father took me to my first movie,
THREE STOOGES MEET SNOW WHITE,
MOE, huge and strange and in color
in the cool darkness after all those years
on the old black-and-white at home,
MOE, shaking his scary black mop of hair,
little pieces of the black air,
MOE, no child, his face strained, damned.

•

CLOSED FOR REPAIRS the sign said one spring,
and we believed it, though we saw no need
for repairs, had taken no notice
of the empty seats. We believed

till the first rocks landed
and the first letters fell,
the shattered marquee glass
raining down. We were no longer children,
though I think we had that look in our eyes.

•

The theater became a tiny shopping mall
with a pizza place, an ice cream place
a drug store and a fabric store
all of which went out of business
to be replaced by other pizza places
an auto parts store a cheap shoe store
and a hot dog shop to be replaced
by a donut place and a hoagie place oh
but no place could fill the cool darkness,
protect us from the bright heat,
the heat of everything.

I can hear you saying *it's only a movie,
only a movie*, but think of stepping out
after the movie ends—for once
it will be raining, and the rain will feel good
on your forehead as you tilt your head back
and close your eyes, your head filled
with what faded off the screen.
Think of rubbing your eyes,
the eyes with no power
except the power of sight.
Think of how you disappeared
there in the dark.

●

We take what shrines the world gives us,
Lord, and I'm afraid to die.
Don't make fun of me
when I take your hand here
where we're a little dead, but mostly alive,
here where the screen unzips itself
and desire steps out,
naked, bright, and beautiful.

SHEDDING THE VESTMENTS

I was inside her for the first time
when her parents pulled up the driveway.

Her father's brain was the size of a small stone
dug up by an idiot pig. He greeted me warmly.

For those brief seconds, I felt the warmth
I would lie and betray and nod and wink

and shuffle and grin and make cheat sheets for,
juggle chainsaws on my unicycle for.

Some of us have a talent for being naked.
Others have a talent for imagining nakedness.

There was nothing gentle about what we did,
frantic explosions under the flashlights of policemen.

Didn't they have something better to do?
When would there ever be anything better to do?

I had a talent for getting lost and making jokes
along the way. Anyone who's going to hell

follow me, I used to say. The teachers ripped
test papers from my hands. I never had

enough time. After that, her mother wouldn't
let me in the house. I stood on the curb

talking to her while her father cut the grass
as short as his hair. We never got that close

again. A stupid boy got her pregnant,
and it wasn't me. I looked at my watch

and sighed. I signed my name to an agreement
to obey traffic signs and crossed myself

as if I believed in something other than
that warmth, that dark wet heaven

that shrunk my brain to the size of a pebble
even that pig would know better than to dig up.

It was me alone in my bed banging my head
against the gates. I am sorry if I disturbed

you, you with something better to do.
You who own the moon's flashlight

and the hammer of dawn. Listen, hear
the zippers falling, the air hissing

out of the slow leak of what we were told
about goodness. Or maybe it's just somebody

alone, remembering and sighing.
Everyone who's following me

go to hell.

NIGHT JANITOR, McMAHON OIL

No one working late tonight. I mean,
except us, but some say we don't work here,
we just clean. Air freshener stinks up

the tiny men's room where lawyers miss, piss
on the floor. I make the steel shine. Jack vacuums
spot theory—he's done in minutes.

I know a few faces here, late-nighters
with their tired smiles. What are they
doing to celebrate this spring evening?

We're going fishing. I steal a roll of toilet paper
for home. Gravel crunches under us in the empty lot.
We spin out. For the hell of it.

Along the banks of the Pine, near Tipton Bridge,
no bass or pike tonight. We catch bluegills,
throw them back.

The company brought in Red Adair once,
the famous oil-fire fighter. Everyone donned hard hats
for pictures with Red to hang on office walls.

There are no pictures with guys holding cleanser,
posed around a toilet, but I'd like to see one of those.
I'd like to see one of those guys piss straight.

•

Jack lost his CETA job working with deaf workers
because there is no CETA anymore. He's taught me
a few signs. *I love this,* he signs. It's nice

that he doesn't have to speak.
Jack gets letters about his loans. They burn like any paper.
I rest my head in my hands and smell cleanser.

Friends passed this job on to us, a couple
who got better jobs and moved on. This job
not enough to live on. We both work days,

minimum wage. *Every three months*
you can steal one can of coffee, our friends said.
We will leave this job as soon as something

comes up. That's a wish. Something
to come up. Tonight I wish my hands smelled
like the river. I let them drag in cold water

but it's not enough. If I catch enough fish
and let them go, my hands will smell like fish.
That's the deal I make tonight. Or maybe just my wish.

•

The fish slide out of my hand and flop back
into the dark river. If I am a fish, I am a bluegill.
If you've ever fished, you've caught a bluegill.

And if it was your first fish, maybe someone let you
keep it, if it was big enough. Most likely
you threw it back. If it didn't swallow the hook.

It's my goal never to swallow the hook.
Jack has to leave soon because he's in love.
She has long blonde hair and paints black canvases,

tends bar at the Pine Knot
and slides us a pitcher or two.
I would like to be in love tonight

but I will settle for my hands smelling like hands.
I will settle for a new roll of toilet paper,
the soft kind, my bonus to myself.

Instead of a cleaning service,
they settled for us. We work cheap, settle
too easily. The office keys rattle in my pocket.

They're alright, the ones I've met,
sweating over figures. Tonight I want
to be generous like the river and let things be.

Before we get in the car, we stand for a moment
and listen to water rushing past below us.
My hands smell a little like fish, a little like cleanser.

I cup them against my face while Jack drives.
You praying again? he says.
It's a joke—he's never seen me pray.

Yeah, I say. I want to make a joke
but I just say *yeah*.

THE FALL

Tonight I look down
from the upstairs window
at the snow angel
I fell to make in the yard
now lit by moonlight,
glistening.

What glorious wings.
What a tiny fucking head.

ST. AGNES AND THE HYPERMARCHÉ

We shop at the hypermarché
in the shadow of the cooling towers
of the nuclear power plant, next to
the cheapest gas station within 100 kilometers.

So, why is the man with the bristly moustache
angry at my children for blocking the aisle
with their miniature shopping carts
with the flags on them?

They are stunned by the size
of the hypermarche´: color tvs and diapers,
suits and herbal remedies at a discount.
Water and wine.

The man bumps my son's cart, and my son and I
turn to stare. Sometimes I still want to punch
someone in the mouth. I try to keep it to myself.

Yesterday, I rode my bike to the tiny chapel
of St. Agnes rising above the river plain,
casting its beautiful lower-case shadow
on empty winter fields, grape vines

cut back to their gnarly core.
Today I fill up at the hypermarché.
This sun makes even the gas pumps glow.

Yesterday I filled myself up at the chapel,
leaning against the locked door,
eyes closed, sun burning through the lids.
I worship the sun of St. Agnes.

I love small things that are beautiful
like my two children. My son looks

like he's going to cry. His preschool teacher
says he's not assertive enough

and should be taking karate.
He's not taking karate, and I'm not
punching anybody. I pull him
to the side. What am I teaching

him? To be a sheep pushing a cart?
I should be shopping at the small stores,
but I can't afford it. Or can I? What
would St. Agnes say?

I pick up some antacids.
Shopping takes forever
with two little kids pushing two little carts.

The only way to do it is to imagine
you have forever. Outside the windows,
the towers look like smoking pistols.
I've been telling secrets to St Agnes

through the thin crack in the old wooden door.
Lighten up, I tell the bristly man, lost pilgrim.
My children are on their way, crashing joyfully
into stacked cookies, paper towels, two for one.

I'm holding onto their flags,
trying to steer through.

HYMNS

Distant trains
   in the Hollow
moan their way into my sleep
       and I vow to be good

   I still remember the words
       to at least a dozen hymns
and my first bitter taste of altar wine
   back in the sanctuary

for years
   I searched for the quick buzz
      and oh yes
I found it
   I won't bore you
   with the names of cheap wines
the places I threw up, passed out

it's good being sober
  though I have been
a good drunk
     I believe in alcohol
       and its spiritual qualities
like I believe in places on a map
      I've never seen

on warm afternoons like today
      a cold glass in my hands
well, I cup it like a prayer
      just a blade of sun slicing through
the small window
    a friend or two

and when I finally leave
to stumble onto a bus toward home
                    the night is spongy and quiet

late nights like this
            I can almost hear my childhood friends
    in their high sing-song voices
                    calling me out again.

SPIDER BOY KILLED AFTER MASSIVE MANHUNT

I opened the door
didn't see a soul
till I looked down
saw a giant spider
the size of a small dog.
Don't believe me, I don't care.

Okay, maybe the size
of a small rat. Maybe it
was a small rat, but it still
doesn't explain who rang the bell
at such a late hour.

Okay, I'd been drinking
tequila on an empty stomach
and had brushed my teeth
with antacid and had held
my breath for five minutes.

Okay, maybe one. I've forgotten
what prompted that, a sour kiss
from a stranger, or simple
self-loathing.

The party was over, and I'd been
holding the telephone
to my forehead for a variety
of reasons. For variety.

I picked up the morning paper
glowing on the dark steps.
That rat's in trouble now,
I remember thinking,
but I turned around
and it was gone.

Blue Jesus

Don't chide me
for my sins. You can chive me
but don't chide me. You can toss me
but don't boss me. It's been so long
since I had a decent salad.

I mourned my way through the news,
dripping tears onto the headlines.
Or maybe I was simply drooling.

It was so sad opening the door
onto the spider boy
when he had nothing to say
and hurried away.
Or maybe he slipped behind me
into the house.

All those swallows and grimaces
and now only this loneliness.
The phone felt cool on my forehead,
soothing with possibility, though
I feel foolish about it now.

3.

BONE AND HOOK

(Triptych, 1981)

1.

Blood trails from beneath the door
like the spray paint of Jesus Christ.

Like an unlit fuse. Like the seventh veil.
And the door is open.

What anyone could see is black
but some of us imagine light

further back.

2.

If my ears had hands, what
would they reach for?
If my knee had a pocket, what
would I store there?

If my toes were tiny flashlights,
I'd still have to crouch to see.

Blood forms a red sheet,
a banner for the worst causes.

I am the poster child
for the willfully deformed
I am the line not to be crossed
I have signed away all rights
I have absolved everyone
of liability.

My spine has been surgically removed.

I've got a box of bodily fluids
ready to mail to the underworld.

A few more orifices couldn't hurt.

3.

My goal is human jello.
The heart my favorite mold.

A foot stretched into taffy.
The handiness of a hook
randomly placed.

Randomness is handy.
I've replaced my spine
with a door jamb.

That window is really
a yield sign.

I've hooked a big one.

The door opens to pure black,
the window to pure light.

I'm standing in the foyer
of the blues, spitting out
my gum and ready to jump.

My toes are melting
and I ain't goin nowhere.

Jesus Christ—He tossed
my bones in the darkness
and said *fetch*.

Blue Jesus

THE BOOGIE-DOWN DANCERS

(Triptych—three studies for a crucifixion, 1962)

The Man in the Middle—
how can we picture Him without
long hair and a beard, the one old hippie
who still goes to all the concerts,
gray streaks in his hair, jeans still hip-
hugging. Shirtless whenever possible.

At any single moment
at least 43 Jesuses exist
in the world. Kinda
franchisey.

No i.d. cards.
Faith is a liability
you can't get insurance for.
Stop me before I get too pithy.

•

Creating facts,
His greatest gift.

There were no thieves
on either side of him—
those were the boogie-down
dancers shakin their thangs.

At what point
did their bodies give in,
drop to the dust?
What music played
in their heads,

the three of them
doing leaps and spins, splits,
Pilate tapping his toes?

RIBS

(Pope II, 1951)

If we're eating His flesh
we may as well slap some
good sauce on it,
fire up the grill.

I mean, who decided on
tasteless wafers,
discarded holes punched
from paper?

How about a bbq on the altar—
priest up there preaching
above the sizzle and smoke.

Save me the gristle.

POPE PULLING A STRING

(Pope I, 1951)

In the dark room
a mirage of faint light
drifts in under the door.

It's important
to wear matching robe
and hat. I'm sure Jesus
said that somewhere.

He looks good in purple.
A small slit of a vacant grin.
One dirty arm raised, gripping
the taut string. It disappears
into darkness. He does not have to
look up—the faith of the blind child
holding what must be a kite
avoiding the wires,
soaring.

SURGERY FOR THE UNDERCLASS

(Painting, 1950)

feelin better
yeah man
feelin better
they turned my nose
into an eraser
kinda tickles yeah
burns a little

but yeah, feelin
on top you know
they cut me in half
but gave me the legs
of the famous dancing mouse
moving slower now
no question about it
but fucking graceful

they turned my ass
into a balloon
but hey they gave me
the string
shitting on myself all day
but hey, it's my shit
if you know what I mean.

TAKING IT FROM BEHIND

(Figure study II, 1945-46)

You can hide under your umbrello
and blanket screaming o Oh OH
but somebody still
eraso your face-o.

Somebody still sneak
under there and
GITCHU
right up the bum
sneak up there
and MESS WIT U

Or if you LIKE that
kinda thing
somebody who KNOW DAT
gon jus SPLAT
you head AGIN the wall

hey hey you
FLABBY-BUTTED
MOTHERFUCKER

belly sagging
like a rotten melon—oh
no—sumpin SQUEAKIN
sumpin ZAPPIN
you with RAYS man

Dat umbrello
turn into a black halo
of bone. Den what?

It so dark WHO KNOWS
what goin on in here
mano mano man

heh heh

and GUESS WHO
got da flashlight?

HAT AND COAT

(Figure study 1, 1945-46)

when all goes limp
when you buy your final
can of worms
only to spill them in the dirt
and watch them roil loose

when you wipe your nose
with a handful of dollar bills
then glue them in your scrapbook

when flowers turn to glass
and the world locks itself
into parallel lines there's no
squeezing between

when the assumption
that smothering yourself
might possibly be for the best

when you disappear without tricks
under your fedora and overcoat
leaving only a large dark lump

when your eulogies are delivered
by the skeletal remains
of what you once called friends

well then.
Yes.

NAKED MAN WITH NEWSPAPER

(Study of George Dyer, 1971)

not reading it
staring away from the window
at the dark wall
it lies at his feet, the world
and its sad announcements
crackling beneath his toes
his mouth ajar
shallow breathing
a shirt waits for him
in another room
and the wristwatch
his father gave him
and a ring he's removed
permanently and a mirror
waiting to forgive him
one more morning

chilled, but still—enough?
he places his hands together
as if in prayer
he lifts them to his lips
and blows.

BLEEDING

(Seated figure, 1962)

dripping on the couch, trailing
into the bathroom, spotting
the tile floor, pressing the cloth
against the nose, tilting back
the head, eyes closed, the dark
wet reminder, grief's dripping
calendar—she's gone gone
gone, swirling paint of bitter words,
maze of unfinished sentences
and in the mirror above the sink
your own eyes shying away
as you suck it back in.

ENORMOUS FOOT

(Triptych, August 1972)

In the world of lower-case
diseases, his stands out proudly,
the Big Dick of diseases. He sits
in his underwear, in the window,
in the sun, smoking his wooden leg,
circling his eyes with ash,

his face smudged with bitterness
and the dead taste of every new thing.
Yesterday he drew a map of his own death.
Today he's creating the algebra.

Why get dressed? Why wear a phony leg?
Why walk? His one remaining foot,
propped up, threatens to float away
like the other one. A cartoon foot swollen
by a dropped safe or a bully's stomp.

His hands disappear under the elastic
of his underwear, though they could do
no harm—there.

The hallway behind him, a black square.
Someone might emerge soon
to wheel him away for some
thing. His flesh holds no secrets.
He's hoping to melt or burn.
Nothing firm, and he's happy
about that.

Behind him, some body
drops some thing. He does not turn
to it. Something falls inside him.
Dismantling, he understands,
is his real job. He knocks
on the wooden leg. He kisses it.

Blue Jesus

MEDITATION ON A NUDE WOMAN WITH SPOTS

(Henrietta Moraes, 1966)

spots where the sun hit
spots where it didn't
spots from a heart's leak
spots from a lover's stain
spots you could swim in
and drown
spots that move in for the kill
spots the cloth could not reach
spots where a stranger sucked blood
spots from a collision in the darkness
spots of fear and desperation
spots from a child's marker
unconnected
spots of dripping shit and bad blood
and kiss it good-bye
spots of sleepless nights and visible
blame, invisible guilt
spots which burn with everything left unsaid
spots which repeat themselves
in the lost hours
spots which cannot be trusted
though you have no choice,
those islands you cannot avoid—
you pray and wait for the crash.

THE BLACK HOLE OF THE HUMAN BODY

(Head II, 1949)

it bore into the leg cast
of a little girl who didn't look
both ways

it was displayed
on the ribs of a bullfighter
and in the open mouths
of the stunned crowd

it appeared as an oil stain
on a gas station calendar
obscuring another
manufactured holiday

the puckered anus
of a bored junkie posing
in a porn magazine

the cancerous lesion
on the cheek
of a self-portrait

the scar of dried snot
pulled from the nose
of the filthy man
with two clean dogs
washing himself
in the playground fountain

it's not going away
so we may as well
plunge our wrists in it

we may as well wave to the shadow
loitering under the streetlight
and call it in.

Blue Jesus

TRIPTYCH: THREE FIGURES AT THE BASE OF A CRUCIFIXION

(Three studies for figures at the base of a crucifixion, 1944)

1. Jesus

Jesus hangs above the swaddled figure
at the base of the cross, no flesh
peeking up to give him a clue.

Is Jesus sulking? Is He bored?
Is He a buzzard hunting new prey?
His head folds into shoulders,
the blades slope toward pain.

A bloody rag eats away
at His feet. Ignore the shadow,
He tells himself.

He sees that the earth
has no seams. It glows red.
No prey in sight, no savior.

2. Guard #1 Speakin'

My butt's sore
from sittin. Think
I'll take a leak.

Long day for the King
of the Jews. Heh heh.

Gotta lose some weight.
Sweatin like a pig.
They gotta make such

a production outta everythin.
Thinkin he's God. *Peek-a-boo,*
Jesus. Crown of thorns,
that was my idea.

Jesus? I been Jesus
myself from time to time.
Think I'll be Jesus tomorrow
as a matter of fact.

I was waitin for him to die.
Didn't want him starin.
Oh man. Nothin better

than takin a piss. Happiest
I been all day.
What you lookin at?

3. Guard #2

He's part dog and part scream,
part joke and part tiger,
part statue and part poison.

His open mouth a howling yawn,
a bored anger. Each step he takes
sears the ground.

He's got tolerance the size of a mole
on his back. And even that's cancerous.

He's got a bulge in his chest
where his heart should be,
but I think it's a big rock.

I know this guy.
He kicked my ass for no reason
except he was bigger.
He likes to show his teeth. I run
when I see those teeth.

But I've never been Jesus, so maybe
I'm not worth the effort. Truth is
I wouldn't have done anything
to try to save Him.
Living with knowing that
keeps the rock in my chest
soft, and beating.

But if I had teeth like that,
who knows.

HAIRCUT ON THE 21ST FLOOR

(Portrait of George Dyer talking, 1966)

My life is a dirty smudge
cultivated into a three-piece suit.
Bless me father, for I have shaved
my grit and made a sand pile
for me to piss in.

I'm part buffalo, part
human virus. I wear a red tie
to hide the fat pill of my sick heart.
I work out every day after work—
poison for poison, I always say.
Do unto others. I have

whenever possible, squeezing
their stringy chicken necks.
That's why I am able
to cover my thinning hair
with pasted dollar bills
and the slick cum of wealth.

My hands, a funnel in my lap
sucking everyone down eventually
while I whisper sweet
nothings.

I always smell nice and squeeze my teeth
into an air-conditioned smile.
The hair on my neck, my only problem.

My wife has lost the power
of speech. She is fragile
as a hollow egg, colored and ornate
outside. I blew out the yolk,
I blew out the white, years ago.

Blue Jesus

I like to rake a comb against my scalp
or better yet, have someone else do it
afternoons like this, my assistant
holding calls, scribbling my signature
on empty sheets of paper.

I used to have to scrape the blood
out from under my nails. No more.
I close my eyes and sigh. *The usual.*

WATER FROM A TAP

(Water from a running tap, 1982)

Dim late-night light
in a public restroom stall,
release easing the strain,
the pressure to go, go,
high windows open
to relieve the stench.

Complex dizzy light
of half-forgotten late-night
dreams half uncovered
by a number of bitter drinks
and prattle.

A head under the tap
cold water running
down the forehead
into the open mouth
into the open hands
the head bent, careful
not to hit the tap

careful and drowning
in what *is no longer
possible*, the lover
had said, the words obscuring
under water left on,
flowing out the open door
into the night.

SNAKED MAN

(Snaked man, 1959)

on the black couch of night
(not its bed)
a man curls his limbs to fit
(a small couch at that)
rubbing his face
into a pillow of chalk.

on the floor beneath him,
his body's outlined
in chalk (limits clearly marked).
he almost glows there,
sleep juice getting sucked
out by the heat. he mops
his chalky brow with a towel,
squeezes out milk into a bowl
and drinks.

(he thinks he's fooling sleep)
he told a wicked lie today
(this is true) he didn't think
he'd have to start paying
for it so soon.

he grabs the rope
(not chalk after all) outlining
his pitiful limbs and gives it
a good shake. it straightens,
then it slithers.

ADAM'S RIBS

(Carcass of meat and bird of prey, 1980)

Slab of ribs hang dripping
in the slaughterhouse,
blood slowly drying into grit.

These pale ribs are the pillars
of all my regrets. Feel the mallet
of my bitter heart, heavy metronome
of my wrecking ball.

The space between bones
is where I live, the space between
a bared claw and a pretty face.
I laugh like a pair of scissors.

My skin peels like bad news.
You will read about me in the space
between lines, between crimes.
I am that meat.

I have captured my own rancid breath
and turned it into a warm breeze
mistaken for harmless.

The spaces between my fingers
are the iron bars of my life.
The spaces between my teeth
are the dark sticks used to make fire.

My sons will kill each other,
as they should.

MAN WITH BLOODY PIG

(Study for portrait on folding bed, 1963)

My nose is the pig's nose.
I've got muscles where the pig's got muscles.

What in this picture does not belong?
Maybe what looks like a pig

is really my bleeding hands wrestling
on my lap. If you look closely

you can see the time on my watch
ticking every woman I've desired.

Don't give me that look. Come on,
guess what I just killed?

It's the red ink of all my bad deals.
It's the hearts smudged off my playing cards—

or the diamonds. My face is chalked
with imaginary cigarette smoke and bad soap.

I'm a monkey's uncle and the pig's
incestuous lover. My tie rises and falls,

rises and falls. *Give up?*
Will you be my new pig?

This is the waiting room
for pain. I will see you now.

Blue Jesus

SPEAKIN OF PHILOSOPHY: THREE STUDIES FROM THE HUMAN BODY

(Three studies from the human body, 1967)

1) a guy swingin on a metal pole,
up and down, round and round.
Very agile, you think.
Looks almost natural doin that.
Why, he's buck naked. He's
a nacherl-born man.

But, see, he's gonna fall.
He can't hold on forever.
Uh-uh. When he fall
into total blackness
all that's left is the pole.
And I mean *total* blackness—
stars is somethin you people dreamed up.

2) this guy, he a floater—
he float and float
in his brown overcoat. He ain't fool
enuff go naked like dat other guy.
He think he's so smart
floatin and floatin

but event-lessly he get bored
then he think he see a little
black spot on his leg.
Uh-oh, he think, I got
the contagion. It juss
a lil ol spot
but he start rubbin and rubbin
tryin to make it go away.

But see, what the dude doin is
he erasin hisself. Floatin

and floatin, rubbin and rubbin
till he juss disappear. His open mouth
the only real black spot. *Well,*
fuck me, those his last words.

3) this guy, he leanin
up agin the wall. He afraid
to jump out onna dat pole.
He bow his head instead. He close
his eyes cause he afraida the pole
when the pole, all dat is
is the thing ya hang onto.

And you know what happen
after a while? He lose
his stickum and fall offa
the wall anyway, never havin
the chance of swingin.

Fallin and fallin, wonderin,
what I do to deserve this?

4) you probly spectin somethin
from me now, kinda
wrap things up.

EVOLUTION: TWO FIGURES WITH MONKEY

(Two figures with a monkey, 1973)

Every light bulb is a hammer
pounding in the regret

of the smudged chalkboard
of last night's blurry

binge that put you here
unclothed and stunned

like that tired wasp
buzzing slow against the window.

The water tap seems impossibly far away.
Our forced smiles crackle at each other.

The tin foil of our brains
tries to unball itself.

Wouldn't it be great if we were
in love? Wouldn't it be great

if that spring wasn't poking through
the mattress? Has anyone ever told you

your hair looks like a dead pheasant?
I didn't know you smoked dynamite.

A monkey walks up the stairs with the mail,
his smile more like a squint, his chattering

more like speech. He carries letters
saying *no* and *give*. He waits

by the side of the bed—gotta buck
for the kid? I ask. Can you do anything

Blue Jesus

about that blue hole in the wall?
you ask. They call that a window, I say.

The monkey vanishes. All that's left
is his tail, a stick floating in blue water.

My head on your quiet chest,
my ear warming. Simultaneous breathing.

Then, wind in the open door
calling us names, everything we deserve.

SELF-PORTRAIT WITH WATCH

(Self-portrait, 1973)

I was grateful once
for light. Tonight I duck

the swinging bulb and chain.
Inside, my brakes squeak,

flakes of rust dropping
with each jolt. The sink

drains slow. I like it that way.
I hold my head in place with one arm.

I've wrestled myself into position.
I'm holding out for natural light.

I've got my running shoes on.
My legs twist into dark wishes.

She isn't coming home.

I like a watch that ticks
like a dripping faucet.

Mine's in my pocket—
it bothers my wrist.

It doesn't tick.
It jabs against my thigh

sarcastic and small.
Sobriety is my favorite

mistake. I dangle one hand
into the sink, washing it

in the dirty air of porcelain
dreams. Soon I'll get out the broom

to sweep up the last stray watts.
In the dark I'll take out my watch

and listen to what passes
for time.

SCREAMING OR YAWNING

(Head VI, 1949)

we all stuck in some kinda clear box
ain't that a hoot or scream
ain't that a finger in a car door

what's filtered out
is the scream, edited out, lost in a box
of colors blended into mud

we got an amusement ride called
the electric chair—how about you?
A monkey's uncle

climbing up the stairs with the mail
speaking in Chinese characters
and you, without your translating glasses

and you, splitting your sleeping pills in half,
bracketing out your dreams, the bass guitar
rumbling into the vacuum cleaner

hi-tech glass, the bulletproof
carousels of liquor stores circling
in the best dreams of lost hope

the roulette wheel of cheap jokes
and discussions about the weather
and you, a man of the cloth

ha, that's a good one
ha, that's a good
one ha that's ha a

ha good ha one—
I lost that final *ha* in a dream
that did not have sex or money in it

Blue Jesus

if you believe that, I've got an electric
toasty thingamabob only driven
once by a state south of the big toe

static smears of a language
you learned for high mass, for low
comedy, for high jinx

Ave Marie, Ave-new,
hokum spokum dippity du
wop wop wop

I'm really
I'm really laughing, busting
a gut—watch out, I'm

crackin up.

JET OF WATER

(Jet of water, 1979)

I am in love
with any fountain
I am promiscuous
with fountains
I have made my wish
I have tossed my coin
I have witnessed the small
splash and gentle sinking

I am in love
with the simplicity
of fountains
water into air
a dribble or a shot
release relief repeat
the mist of vague dreams

let me take you there
(let me take you there)
lit by evening and fragile sin
(lit by the one forgiving eye)
and if we wade in the pool
(and if we wade in the pool)
will we receive a saving grace
(will we give a saving grace)

oh Lord when I die
(when I die)
leave the water running